Finance
Your Own
Film

For Filmmakers on a Budget

CHRIS G. WENCHELL

"Independent filmmaking, like independent voices, has the power to challenge the status quo and change the world."

-   *Robert Redford*

Finance Your Own Film: For Filmmakers on a Budget

I. Introduction
  A. Overview of the Challenges Filmmakers Face in Financing Their Own Projects.
  B. Importance of Understanding Financing Options and Strategies for Independent Filmmakers.

II. Understanding the Landscape
  A. Overview of the Film Industry and It's Various Sectors.
  B. The Role of Budgeting and Financing in Successful Film Production.
  C. The Difference Between Studio-Funded and Independent Film Projects.

III. Key Lessons from "The Complete Film Production Handbook"
  A. Understanding the Fundamentals of Film Production, Including Financing and Budgeting.
  B. The Essential Steps and Considerations in Fundraising for a Film Project.
  C. The Importance of Effective Management Throughout the Production Process.

IV. Exploring Financing Options
  A. Traditional Funding Sources.
    i.   Grants and Film Funds.
    ii. Investors and Production Companies.
    iii. Film Festivals and Competitions.
  B. Alternative Funding and DIY Strategies.
    i.   Crowdfunding (e.g., Kickstarter, Indiegogo).
    ii. Self-Financing and Personal Savings.
    iii. Pre-sales and Distribution Deals.
    iv. Tax Incentives and Rebates.
    v.   Co-Production and Partnerships.
    vi. Product Placement and Brand Integration.

XI.   Insurance and Risk Management
    A. Understanding Types of Insurance for Risk Mitigation During Production.

XII.   Pre-visualization and Storyboarding
    A. Utilizing Pre-Visualization and Storyboarding for Visualization and Presentation.

XIII.   Market Research and Audience Analysis
    A. Conducting Market Research and Understanding the Target Audience.

XIV.   Film Festivals and Networking
    A. Utilizing Film Festivals and Networking Events for Opportunities and Funding.

XV.   Digital Distribution and Online Platforms
    A. Leveraging Digital Distribution and Online Platforms for Audience Engagement and Revenue Generation.

XVI.   Ethical and Sustainable Financing Practices
    A. Promoting Ethical and Sustainable Financing Practices in the Film Industry.

XVII.   Conclusion
    A. Reiterating the Importance of Proper Financing and Budgeting for Successful Film Projects.
    B. Encouragement for Filmmakers to Explore Various. Financing Options and Embrace Creativity in Funding Their Projects.
    C. Encouraging Continuous Learning and Networking within The Film Industry.

Preface

Lights, camera, action! There's an undeniable magic in the world of filmmaking. It's a realm where stories come alive, emotions are captured, and dreams take shape on the silver screen. Yet, for many aspiring filmmakers, there's a challenge that often stands as a formidable roadblock on this creative journey—financing.

Filmmaking is an art, a craft, and a labor of love. It's about bringing visions to life, sharing stories that matter, and leaving an indelible mark on the world. But it's also a venture that demands resources—financial resources. And for those who are passionate about their craft but find their budgets limited, this challenge can feel like an insurmountable wall.

This book, "Finance Your Own Film for Filmmakers on a Budget," is your key to unlock that door. It's a guide for dreamers and doers, for storytellers who refuse to be bound by financial constraints. Here, we embark on a journey that takes you from a vision to a masterpiece, and along the way, we'll learn the art of resourcefulness.

We delve into budgeting, dissecting the anatomy of a film's financial needs. We explore the dynamic landscape of financing, uncovering traditional methods, and embracing innovative approaches, such as crowdfunding and partnerships. We master the skill of presenting your project to investors and sponsors, turning your vision into an irresistible proposition.

But this book isn't just about the numbers. It's also about the spirit. The stories shared within these pages, the tales of filmmakers who, like you, had dreams and ambitions, who faced limitations and yet found their way to bring their projects to life— these are your companions on this journey.

We also navigate the legal terrain, ensuring that you're equipped with the knowledge to protect your work and your investments. We discuss the vital role of effective management in keeping your project on course and on time. And we consider the ever-expanding universe of digital distribution and audience engagement, where new possibilities for independent filmmakers continue to emerge.

"Finance Your Own Film for Filmmakers on a Budget" is more than a book; it's your ally, your confidant, and your guide. It's your ticket to realizing your cinematic dreams within financial constraints. It's an invitation to creativity, perseverance, and the belief that, with the right knowledge and the right mindset, you can achieve your cinematic aspirations.

So, fellow filmmaker, as you turn the page, remember that your journey is unique, and this book is your companion. Let's embrace the art of resourcefulness, redefine the boundaries of possibility, and bring your cinematic dreams to life. The world is waiting for your story, and we're here to help you share it.

Now, let's make your dreams a reality. Let's begin the journey.

Onward, to the world of limitless cinematic possibilities.

Chapter I: Introduction

Finance Your Own Film: For Filmmakers on a Budget

In this introductory chapter, we will explore the significant challenges that filmmakers encounter when seeking to finance their projects. We'll highlight the crucial importance of understanding various financing options and strategies, particularly for independent filmmakers striving to bring their creative visions to life.

A. Overview of the Challenges Filmmakers Face in Financing Their Own Projects

The path to creating a film is often fraught with financial challenges. Filmmakers, especially independent ones, face numerous hurdles when it comes to financing their projects:

- Funding Limitations: Independent filmmakers often operate on limited budgets, restricting the scale and ambition of their projects. Securing adequate funds for pre-production, production, post-production, marketing, and distribution can be an arduous task.

- Competitive Landscape: The film industry is highly competitive, making it difficult for emerging filmmakers to secure funding. There's intense competition for grants, investors, and other financial opportunities. Standing out in this competitive landscape requires a well-crafted strategy and a unique value proposition.

- **Risk and Uncertainty:** Filmmaking involves inherent risks, and investors may be hesitant to commit funds to projects with uncertain returns. Mitigating these risks and providing assurances to investors is a crucial aspect of fundraising. This requires understanding market trends, audience preferences, and effective communication of the project's potential.

B. Importance of Understanding Financing Options and Strategies for Independent Filmmakers

Understanding the vast array of financing options and strategies available is pivotal for independent filmmakers for several reasons:

- **Empowerment through Knowledge:** Knowledge of various financing avenues empowers filmmakers to make informed decisions about how to fund their projects. It allows them to tailor their approach based on the nature of the film, the target audience, and market trends.

- **Adaptability and Resourcefulness:** Awareness of multiple funding strategies enables filmmakers to adapt to different circumstances. They can explore a combination of funding sources, adapt their financial models, and utilize creative fundraising approaches.

- **Sustainable Filmmaking Career:** Acquiring knowledge about financing lays the foundation for a sustainable filmmaking career. Filmmakers can navigate the industry landscape, build relationships with investors, and make informed choices that can lead to successful projects and future collaborations.

C. The Journey Ahead

In the subsequent chapters, we will delve deeper into various financing options and strategies tailored to the needs of independent filmmakers. We'll explore grants, crowdfunding, investors, and other funding sources. We'll discuss effective budgeting techniques and financial planning, providing valuable insights to overcome these challenges and embark on a successful filmmaking journey.

Conclusion

The challenges filmmakers face in financing their projects are daunting, but understanding the financial landscape and having a repertoire of strategies at their disposal can make a significant difference. Join us as we explore the diverse avenues of film financing, empowering filmmakers to navigate the financial landscape and bring their creative visions to fruition.

Chapter II: Understanding the Landscape

In this chapter, we will delve into an understanding of the film industry's diverse sectors and dynamics. We'll emphasize the pivotal role of budgeting and financing in achieving successful film production. Additionally, we'll distinguish between studio-funded and independent film projects, shedding light on their unique characteristics and challenges.

A. Overview of the Film Industry and Its Various Sectors

The film industry is a multifaceted realm encompassing various sectors that collectively contribute to the creation, distribution, and exhibition of films.

- **Production Sector:** Involves the actual making of films, encompassing pre-production, production, and post-production phases. This sector brings together directors, producers, writers, actors, crew members, and post-production teams to breathe life into a film project.

- **Distribution Sector:** Focuses on marketing, selling, and delivering films to audiences. Distributors play a key role in strategizing release plans, negotiating deals, and ensuring films reach their intended viewers through theaters, streaming platforms, DVDs, or television.

- Exhibition Sector: Involves the presentation of films to audiences, primarily through cinemas or movie theaters. It's the venue where audiences experience films on the big screen, contributing to the industry's revenue stream.

- Marketing and Promotion: Encompasses strategies to create awareness and generate interest in a film. This sector utilizes various marketing channels, including digital platforms, advertisements, trailers, press releases, and promotional events.

B. The Role of Budgeting and Financing in Successful Film Production

Budgeting and financing are linchpins in the film production process, influencing every stage of filmmaking.

- Budgeting: Involves the allocation of funds for various aspects of the film, encompassing pre-production, production, post-production, marketing, and distribution. A well-structured budget ensures efficient resource allocation and helps in managing costs throughout the project. Detailed budgeting helps in understanding the financial requirements for each stage and aids in decision-making.

- Financing: Refers to securing the necessary funds to cover the budgeted expenses. Filmmakers explore diverse funding sources such as grants, loans, investors, crowdfunding, sponsorships, and pre-sales to finance their projects. Effective financing is critical for bringing the creative vision to life. It involves crafting a clear financial plan and approaching potential funders strategically.

- Challenges and Strategies: Acknowledging the challenges filmmakers face in securing funding, including competition for grants and the need for a compelling pitch. Strategies such as building relationships with investors, leveraging networking opportunities, and demonstrating the film's potential for returns can significantly aid in overcoming these challenges.

C. The Difference Between Studio-Funded and Independent Film Projects

Understanding the distinction between studio-funded and independent film projects is vital for filmmakers navigating the industry landscape.

- **Studio-Funded Films:** Typically financed and produced by major film studios. These films often have substantial budgets, extensive resources, established distribution networks, and are associated with well-known directors, producers, and actors. Studio-funded projects benefit from wider marketing reach and broad theatrical releases. However, they may face creative constraints due to commercial considerations.

- **Independent Films:** Produced outside the major studio system. Independent filmmakers often operate on smaller budgets, relying on creativity, innovation, and passion. These films may target niche audiences, have limited marketing resources, and may opt for selective theatrical releases or primarily digital distribution platforms. Independent films offer creative freedom but require resourcefulness and effective marketing strategies.

Conclusion

Understanding the landscape of the film industry is paramount for filmmakers aiming to navigate its complexities effectively. Recognizing the sectors, comprehending the role of budgeting and financing, and discerning the dynamics between studio-funded and independent projects lay a solid foundation for a successful filmmaking journey.

Chapter III: Key Lessons from "The Complete Film Production Handbook"

In this chapter, we will distill essential lessons from "The Complete Film Production Handbook," focusing on understanding the fundamental aspects of film production, emphasizing financing and budgeting, discussing the critical steps in fundraising, and recognizing the paramount importance of effective management throughout the production process.

A. Understanding the Fundamentals of Film Production

Film production encompasses a broad spectrum of crucial elements, and grasping these fundamentals is vital for any filmmaker:

- **Pre-production Essentials:** Discussing the importance of thorough pre-production, including script development, storyboarding, casting, location scouting, and creating a production timeline. Emphasizing how a solid pre-production foundation sets the stage for a successful film.

- **Production Techniques:** Exploring fundamental production techniques such as cinematography, lighting, sound recording, and directing. Highlighting how mastering these techniques is integral to creating a visually and acoustically appealing film.

- **Post-production Dynamics:** Delving into the post-production phase, covering editing, special effects, sound design, and scoring. Emphasizing the role of post-production in enhancing the overall quality and impact of the film.

- **Collaboration and Team Dynamics:** Stressing the importance of teamwork and effective collaboration among various departments in a film production. Discussing how a cohesive and well-coordinated team significantly contributes to the success of a film.

B. The Essential Steps and Considerations in Fundraising for a Film Project

Fundraising is a pivotal aspect of film production, and understanding the steps and considerations involved is crucial:

- **Defining Budget Requirements:** Discussing how to conduct a comprehensive assessment of the financial needs of a film project, considering all aspects from pre-production to distribution. Emphasizing the importance of creating a detailed and accurate budget.

- **Fundraising Strategies:** Exploring various strategies for fundraising, such as grants, investors, crowdfunding, and sponsorships. Discussing the pros and cons of each approach and when to utilize them based on the project's requirements.

- **Pitching and Presenting:** Providing guidance on how to create an effective pitch or presentation to attract potential investors or donors. Discussing the elements of a compelling pitch, including the storyline, target audience, and financial projections.

- **Relationship Building with Investors:** Stressing the significance of building and maintaining strong relationships with investors and donors. Discussing how trust and credibility play a crucial role in securing funding for the project.

C. The Importance of Effective Management Throughout the Production Process

Efficient management is key to the success of any film project. This section focuses on effective management practices:

- **Project Management Principles:** Discussing fundamental project management principles and methodologies that can be applied to film production. Emphasizing the importance of organization, planning, and coordination throughout the production cycle.

- **Team Collaboration and Communication:** Highlighting the significance of seamless collaboration and effective communication within the production team. Discussing strategies to ensure a cohesive and productive work environment.

- **Risk Management and Contingency Planning:** Discussing how to identify potential risks in a film project and develop strategies to mitigate them. Emphasizing the need for contingency plans to handle unexpected challenges that may arise during production.

- **Time Management and Scheduling:** Addressing the importance of efficient time management and scheduling in film production. Discussing how adhering to timelines and deadlines is crucial for the successful completion of the project.

Conclusion

"The Complete Film Production Handbook" offers invaluable lessons for filmmakers, emphasizing the significance of understanding film production fundamentals, effective fundraising, and efficient project management. Grasping these lessons equips filmmakers with the knowledge and tools necessary to navigate the multifaceted world of film production successfully.

Chapter IV: Exploring Financing Options

In this chapter, we will explore a wide array of financing options available to filmmakers, ranging from traditional sources to innovative DIY strategies. Understanding these options is essential for filmmakers seeking to secure funding for their projects.

A. Traditional Funding Sources

Traditional funding sources are foundational avenues for financing a film project:

Grants and Film Funds

- **Understanding Grants:** Delving into the concept of grants and how they provide funds to filmmakers based on specific criteria such as the project's theme, region, or social impact. Discussing the importance of a well-structured proposal when applying for grants.
- **Film Funds:** Exploring film funds, which are financial resources set up to support the production of films. Discussing how filmmakers can access these funds, the application process, and the varying requirements of different film funds.
- **Application Strategies:** Providing tips and strategies on how to write a compelling grant application, including elements such as project synopsis, budget breakdown, and the impact of the film.

Investors and Production Companies

- **Investor Relations:** Discussing the relationship between filmmakers and investors. Exploring how filmmakers can attract investors, pitch their projects, negotiate terms, and maintain strong investor relations throughout the production.
- **Production Companies:** Exploring partnerships with production companies and their role in financing film projects. Discussing how to approach production companies, negotiate deals, and collaborate effectively to secure funding.
- **Negotiation Skills:** Providing insights into effective negotiation skills that filmmakers can employ when dealing with investors or production companies. Discussing strategies to negotiate for better terms and conditions.

Film Festivals and Competitions

- **Film Festival Funding:** Discussing how film festivals can provide financial support to filmmakers through grants, prizes, or sponsorships. Exploring strategies for identifying and applying to festivals that offer funding opportunities.
- **Competitions and Awards:** Exploring how competitions and awards within film festivals can provide financial rewards or resources to further develop a project. Discussing how filmmakers can strategically participate in these competitions.
- **Networking at Festivals:** Providing guidance on how filmmakers can effectively network at film festivals to build relationships that might lead to funding opportunities.

B. Alternative Funding and DIY Strategies

Alternative funding and DIY strategies offer creative and innovative approaches to financing a film project:

Crowdfunding (e.g., Kickstarter, Indiegogo)

- **Crowdfunding Platforms:** Introducing popular crowdfunding platforms like Kickstarter and Indiegogo. Discussing how filmmakers can create compelling campaigns, set fundraising goals, and engage with their audience to successfully fund their projects.
- **Campaign Planning:** Providing a step-by-step guide on how to plan a successful crowdfunding campaign, including creating engaging content, setting rewards, and setting a realistic funding goal.

Self-Financing and Personal Savings

- **Self-Financing Strategies:** Discussing how filmmakers can use their personal savings or assets to fund their projects. Exploring the pros and cons of self-financing and strategies to manage risks associated with this approach.
- **Budgeting for Self-Financing:** Providing insights into budgeting strategies for filmmakers who choose to self-finance, ensuring they allocate resources effectively and maintain financial stability throughout the project.

Pre-sales and Distribution Deals

- **Pre-sales and Distribution Agreements:** Exploring the concept of pre-sales where filmmakers secure funding by selling distribution rights in advance. Discussing the importance of a strong script and marketing strategy to attract potential buyers.
- **Negotiating Distribution Deals:** Offering negotiation tips and strategies for filmmakers seeking pre-sales or distribution deals, ensuring they get the best terms and maximize financial gains.

Tax Incentives and Rebates

- **Tax Incentives:** Discussing how filmmakers can benefit from tax incentives provided by governments or specific regions to encourage filmmaking. Exploring the eligibility criteria and application process for these incentives.

- Maximizing Tax Benefits: Providing advice on how filmmakers can maximize tax benefits by understanding tax laws and utilizing incentives effectively.

Co-Production and Partnerships

- Co-Production Strategies: Exploring the benefits of co-producing a film with other filmmakers or production companies. Discussing how co-production can provide access to additional funds, resources, and expertise.

- Navigating Co-Production Agreements: Discussing how filmmakers can navigate co-production agreements, outlining responsibilities, financial contributions, and revenue-sharing arrangements.

Product Placement and Brand Integration

- Product Placement Strategies: Discussing how filmmakers can integrate products and brands into their films for financial support. Exploring the negotiation process, legal considerations, and the potential benefits of this approach.

- Building Brand Partnerships: Providing guidance on how filmmakers can establish successful partnerships with brands for product placement, ensuring a win-win situation for both parties.

Film Grants and Fellowships

- Film Grants and Fellowships: Delving into specific grants and fellowship opportunities available to filmmakers. Discussing the application process, eligibility criteria, and how filmmakers can maximize their chances of receiving funding.

- Crafting a Winning Application: Offering advice on how to craft a compelling application for grants and fellowships, showcasing the project's uniqueness and its potential impact.

Conclusion

Understanding the diverse financing options available is a pivotal step for filmmakers aiming to fund their projects successfully. From traditional sources such as grants and investors to innovative DIY strategies like crowdfunding and product placement, each avenue offers unique advantages and challenges.

Chapter V: Budgeting and Financial Management

In this chapter, we'll explore the critical aspects of budgeting and financial management in filmmaking. Understanding how to create a detailed film budget, effectively track expenses, and adapt budgets to various funding levels are essential skills for filmmakers to successfully manage their projects.

A. Creating a Detailed Film Budget

Creating a thorough and accurate film budget is a fundamental step in managing a film project effectively:

- **Breakdown of Costs:** Discussing the comprehensive breakdown of costs involved in filmmaking, including pre-production, production, post-production, marketing, and distribution. Highlighting the importance of meticulously identifying and estimating expenses in each stage.

- **Budgeting Software and Tools:** Introducing filmmakers to budgeting software and tools that can aid in creating and managing budgets efficiently. Providing insights into how these tools can streamline the budgeting process and ensure accuracy.

- **Contingency Planning:** Stressing the need for contingency funds within the budget to handle unexpected expenses or emergencies. Exploring the concept of 'padding' and its significance in ensuring a project stays within budget.

- Allocation and Prioritization: Discussing how to allocate the budget based on the project's needs and priorities. Emphasizing the importance of allocating funds according to the project's vision, potential return on investment, and critical aspects of production.

B. Tracking Expenses and Controlling Costs

Efficiently tracking expenses and maintaining cost control is vital for the financial health of a film project:

- Expense Tracking Systems: Exploring various methods and systems to track expenses during production. Discussing the importance of real-time expense tracking and its role in maintaining financial discipline.

- Cost Control Strategies: Providing strategies to control costs during the different phases of the film project. Emphasizing efficient resource allocation, negotiating favorable contracts, and minimizing unnecessary expenditures.

- Financial Reporting and Analysis: Introducing filmmakers to financial reporting techniques that allow for a detailed analysis of expenses. Discussing how such analysis can guide decision-making and help in optimizing budget allocation.

- Monitoring Budget Performance: Emphasizing the need for regular monitoring of the budget's performance throughout the project. Discussing strategies to address budget deviations and ensure the project stays on financial track.

C. Adapting Budgets to Funding Levels

Adapting budgets based on the available funding is crucial for project sustainability and success:

- Tiered Budgeting: Explaining the concept of tiered budgeting, where filmmakers create budgets for different funding levels. Discussing how this flexibility allows for seamless adjustments as funding levels fluctuate.

- Scaling Production Needs: Demonstrating how to scale production needs based on the available funds. Discussing strategies to prioritize essential elements while adjusting others based on the project's financial capacity.

- Maintaining Quality Standards: Emphasizing the need to maintain quality standards even when working with limited funds. Providing insights into creative solutions and efficient resource allocation that ensure a high-quality production despite budget constraints.

- Revising the Budget Strategically: Discussing when and how to strategically revise the budget based on new funding opportunities, unexpected expenses, or changes in the project's scope.

Conclusion

Budgeting and financial management are the backbone of a successful film project. Understanding how to create a detailed budget, track expenses, control costs, and adapt budgets to varying funding levels is pivotal. These skills empower filmmakers to manage their resources effectively, ultimately bringing their creative visions to life within the confines of their financial means.

Chapter VI: Key Lessons from "Independent Feature Film Production"

In this chapter, we will extract valuable lessons from "Independent Feature Film Production," shedding light on the diverse funding sources available to independent filmmakers. We'll also explore practical tips for navigating the intricate landscape of the film industry, emphasizing the role of perseverance and creativity in securing financing for film projects.

A. Insights into Traditional and Alternative Funding Sources for Independent Filmmakers

Securing funding is a critical step in realizing an independent film project. "Independent Feature Film Production" offers insights into a spectrum of funding options:

- **Traditional Funding Sources:** Exploring avenues such as grants, loans, and investment from production companies or private investors. These conventional sources provide financial stability and support, but often come with specific requirements and considerations. Understanding how to craft compelling proposals and presentations for potential investors and applying for grants is vital.

- **Crowdfunding:** Delving into the world of crowdfunding platforms where filmmakers can directly connect with their audience to fund their projects. This approach empowers filmmakers to pitch their ideas, garner support, and raise funds from a broad community of backers. The book might elaborate on successful crowdfunding campaigns, strategies to create engaging campaigns, and the importance of offering enticing rewards.

- **Sponsorships and Product Placement:** Understanding how strategic partnerships and product placements can serve as funding sources. Filmmakers can collaborate with brands and companies to integrate products into their films, generating revenue and resources for production. The book could provide case studies or examples of successful integrations and how filmmakers can approach potential sponsors.

B. Practical Tips for Navigating the Complexities of the Film Industry

The film industry is a complex ecosystem with various stages and intricacies. "Independent Feature Film Production" offers practical advice on how to navigate this landscape effectively:

- **Effective Networking:** Stressing the importance of networking within the industry. Building relationships with fellow filmmakers, producers, investors, and professionals can open doors to opportunities, collaborations, and potential funding avenues. The book might elaborate on networking strategies, attending industry events, and leveraging social media.

- **Understanding Distribution Channels:** Providing insights into the diverse distribution channels available, including theatrical releases, streaming platforms, and film festivals. Understanding how to strategically position and distribute a film is crucial for success. This could include strategies for submitting to film festivals, negotiating with distributors, and utilizing online platforms effectively.

- Market Research and Audience Targeting: Emphasizing the significance of understanding the target audience and conducting thorough market research. Knowing the preferences and demands of the audience aids in shaping the film and marketing it effectively. The book might delve into techniques for audience analysis, focus groups, and leveraging digital tools for market research.

C. Understanding the Importance of Perseverance and Creativity in Securing Financing

Perseverance and creativity are essential qualities for independent filmmakers aiming to secure financing:

- Perseverance: Encouraging filmmakers to persist in their efforts to secure funding. Rejections and challenges are part of the journey, but perseverance can turn setbacks into stepping stones towards success. The book could include motivational stories of filmmakers who faced rejection but persisted and ultimately succeeded.

- Creativity in Fundraising: Highlighting the need for creativity not only in filmmaking but also in fundraising. Thinking outside the box and exploring unconventional funding methods can make a project stand out and attract potential investors. This section could provide innovative fundraising ideas and success stories from filmmakers who employed creative financing strategies.

Conclusion

"Independent Feature Film Production" provides invaluable lessons for independent filmmakers navigating the complex world of film financing. Understanding the diverse funding sources, practical industry tips, and the importance of perseverance and creativity are fundamental to achieving success in the fiercely competitive realm of independent filmmaking.

Chapter VII: Marketing and Promotion for Funding

A. Building a Strong Online Presence

Building a robust online presence is essential for attracting funding and support for film projects. In this section, we'll explore how filmmakers can establish and optimize their presence on the internet.

Creating an Engaging Website

- **Professional Portfolio:** Showcasing past projects, credentials, and expertise to instill confidence in potential backers.
    - **Key Lessons:** A well-organized portfolio demonstrates professionalism and allows potential backers to understand the filmmaker's capabilities.
- **Contact Information:** Providing clear and easily accessible contact details for inquiries and collaboration opportunities.
    - **Key Lessons:** Easy-to-find contact information ensures interested parties can reach out easily, fostering potential collaborations and funding opportunities.

Engaging with an Audience through Blogging

- **Content Relevance:** Creating informative and engaging blog posts related to filmmaking, industry trends, and project updates.

- Key Lessons: Relevant and insightful blog content attracts a dedicated audience, establishing the filmmaker as an authority in their field.

- Interactive Engagement: Encouraging audience interaction through comments, discussions, and feedback.

- Key Lessons: Engaging with the audience fosters a sense of community and increases the visibility of the filmmaker and their projects.

B. Leveraging Social Media and Digital Marketing

Social media and digital marketing are powerful tools for attracting attention and funding. This section explores strategies to effectively utilize these platforms.

Strategic Social Media Use

- Platform Selection: Identifying and focusing on platforms where the project's target audience is most active.

- Key Lessons: Understanding the target audience's preferred platforms enables targeted marketing efforts and better engagement.

- Consistent Engagement: Regularly interacting with the audience through posts, updates, and responding to comments.

- Key Lessons: Consistency in engagement builds a loyal following, increasing the project's visibility and potential for funding.

Harnessing the Power of Email Marketing

- Building a Subscriber List: Encouraging website visitors and social media followers to subscribe for updates and newsletters.

- Key Lessons: Building a strong email list provides a direct channel to potential backers and supporters, keeping them informed and engaged.

- **Personalized Campaigns:** Sending personalized and targeted emails to keep the audience informed about the project's progress and funding campaigns.
    - **Key Lessons:** Personalization increases engagement and the likelihood of support, making each supporter feel valued and connected to the project.

C. Showcasing Previous Work and Achievements

Showcasing previous work and achievements is a potent strategy for garnering support and funding for upcoming projects. In this section, we'll explore how filmmakers can effectively showcase their track record.

Compiling a Strong Portfolio

- **Highlighting Key Projects**: Showcasing successful and well-received projects prominently within the portfolio.
    - **Key Lessons:** Emphasizing successful projects establishes credibility and showcases the filmmaker's capabilities.
- **Testimonials and Reviews:** Including testimonials and reviews from collaborators, actors, and critics to add credibility.
    - **Key Lessons:** Authentic testimonials provide social proof, reinforcing the filmmaker's skills and professionalism.

Participation in Film Festivals and Competitions

- **Listing Achievements:** Displaying awards, nominations, or official selections in renowned film festivals and competitions.
    - **Key Lessons:** Listing achievements enhances credibility and attracts attention from potential backers and industry professionals.
- **Sharing Experiences:** Providing insights and reflections on the experiences and lessons learned from participating in various events.

- **Key Lessons:** Sharing experiences offers a glimpse into the filmmaker's journey, creating a personal connection with the audience.

D. Case Studies: Successful Marketing Strategies for Funding

In this section, we analyze real-life case studies that showcase successful marketing and promotional strategies employed by filmmakers to secure funding for their projects.

Case Study 1: Engaging Online Community

- **Campaign Overview:** Detailing a successful online community engagement campaign, highlighting strategies that drove engagement and funding support.
- **Key Lessons:** Building an engaged online community can lead to significant support and funding, showcasing the power of audience engagement.
- **Key Takeaways:** Extracting essential lessons from the case study to guide filmmakers in building an engaged online community for funding.
- **Key Lessons:** Consistency in engagement builds a loyal following, increasing the project's visibility and potential for funding.

Case Study 2: Effective Digital Advertising Campaign

- **Campaign Strategy:** Analyzing a case where an effective digital advertising campaign significantly impacted the project's funding success.
- **Key Lessons:** A well-planned digital advertising campaign can effectively reach a broader audience, driving support and funding for the project.

- Lessons Learned: Identifying the key lessons from the case study to assist filmmakers in creating impactful digital advertising strategies for funding.

> **- Key Lessons:** Effective digital advertising requires targeting, compelling content, and strategic placement to maximize engagement and conversions.

This chapter underscores the importance of marketing and promotion in securing funding for film projects. By effectively leveraging a strong online presence, social media engagement, and showcasing past work and achievements, filmmakers can enhance their project's visibility and attract the financial support needed to bring their creative visions to fruition.

Chapter VIII: Real-Life Experiences

In this chapter, we'll delve into real-life experiences of filmmakers in securing funding for their film projects and explore effective networking and relationship-building strategies within the industry.

A. Learning from Real-Life Experiences in Securing Funding

In the dynamic world of film financing, learning from the experiences of other filmmakers is invaluable. Real-life stories shed light on the challenges and triumphs encountered during the funding journey.

Story of Independent Filmmaker A

- **Challenges Faced:** Facing initial rejections and struggling to find investors willing to take a chance on a debut project.
- **Approaches Taken:** Utilizing personal savings, crowdfunding, and grants from film institutions to piece together the necessary funds.
- **Key Lessons:**
    - **Persistence Pays Off:** Persevering through rejections and setbacks can eventually lead to finding the right funding sources.
    - **Diversify Funding Streams:** Relying on a mix of funding sources can provide a safety net and improve the overall financial stability of the project.

Story of Emerging Filmmaker B

- **Challenges Faced:** Wrestling with limited industry connections and struggling to gain traction for the project.
- **Approaches Taken**: Actively networking at industry events, leveraging social media to showcase the project, and forming partnerships with like-minded filmmakers.
- **Key Lessons:**
    - **Network with Purpose:** Building relationships within the industry is crucial, and it's essential to have a clear strategy and objectives when networking.
    - **Collaboration is Key:** Partnering with others can amplify your project's visibility and open doors to funding opportunities that may not be accessible individually.

B. Strategies for Effective Networking and Relationship-Building

Building strong relationships within the film industry can significantly impact your ability to secure funding and advance your projects.

Building Genuine Relationships

- **Approach to Networking:** Approaching networking with a genuine interest in others, their projects, and a willingness to offer help or support.
- **Key Strategies:**
    - **Active Listening:** Actively listening to others and showing genuine interest in what they have to say fosters meaningful connections.
    - **Reciprocity:** Offering assistance or value before expecting something in return is a fundamental principle in building lasting relationships.

Utilizing Industry Events and Platforms

- Participation Strategies: Strategically selecting and participating in industry events that align with your project's genre or theme.
- Key Takeaways:
>**- Targeted Participation:** Focusing on events that attract potential investors, distributors, or collaborators increases the chances of meaningful connections.
>**- Online Presence:** Extending your network through online platforms, such as LinkedIn or film industry forums, can complement in-person networking efforts.

C. The Importance of a Well-Prepared Pitch

A compelling pitch is often the gateway to securing funding for your film project.

Crafting a Compelling Pitch

- Essential Elements:
>**- A Captivating Story:** Ensuring that your pitch narrates your film's story effectively, conveying its unique elements and appeal.
>**- Clear Budget Breakdown:** Clearly outlining how the funds will be utilized and the expected outcomes.
>**- Passion and Conviction:** Delivering the pitch with enthusiasm and confidence, demonstrating your commitment to the project.

- Pitch Preparation Tips:
>**- Practice Makes Perfect:** Rehearsing your pitch numerous times helps you become more comfortable and polished in delivering it.
>**- Feedback and Iteration:** Seeking feedback from trusted industry peers and refining your pitch based on their insights.

- Key Success Factors:

- Alignment with Investor Goals: Tailoring your pitch to resonate with the specific goals and preferences of the potential investors you're addressing.

By exploring real-life experiences in securing funding for film projects, understanding effective networking strategies, and emphasizing the importance of a well-prepared pitch, filmmakers can enhance their abilities to connect with potential investors and navigate the financing landscape successfully.

Chapter IX: Legal and Contractual Considerations in Film Financing

In this chapter, we'll delve into essential legal and contractual aspects that filmmakers need to consider when navigating the complex landscape of film financing.

A. Contracts and Agreements with Investors

When securing funding for your film project, clear and well-drafted contracts and agreements are crucial to protect both parties involved.

Comprehensive Investment Contracts

- **Key Components:** Detailing the terms of the investment, return on investment, equity or profit-sharing agreements, and the investor's involvement in decision-making processes.
- **Risk Mitigation:** Outlining the risks associated with the investment, clarifying the investor's potential losses and the extent of liability.

Transparency and Clarity

- **Legal Language Simplified:** Ensuring that contracts are written in a clear, understandable manner to prevent misinterpretation or disputes.
- **Mutual Understanding**: Confirming that all parties involved fully comprehend and agree to the terms laid out in the contracts.

Legal Review and Approval

- **Consulting Legal Professionals:** Advising filmmakers to seek legal counsel to review contracts before signing, ensuring they protect the filmmaker's interests.
- Negotiation Skills: Developing negotiation skills to effectively discuss terms with investors and draft contracts that are fair and balanced.

B. Intellectual Property Rights and Copyrights

Protecting your intellectual property is paramount in the film industry, where creativity and originality are highly valued.

Securing Copyrights

- **Registration Process:** Familiarizing yourself with the copyright registration process to protect your screenplay, film content, music, and other creative elements.
- **Ownership Clarification:** Clearly specifying the ownership of intellectual property in contracts to avoid conflicts.

Licensing and Permissions

- **Permissions for Use:** Ensuring proper licensing and permissions for any copyrighted material, including music, artwork, or written content used in the film.
- **Release Forms:** Acquiring signed release forms from actors, crew, and other contributors to the film, granting permission to use their likeness, performances, or work.

Trademark and Brand Protection

- **Trademark Registration:** Considering trademark registration for the film title, logo, or any distinctive brand elements associated with the project.
- **Avoiding Infringement:** Conducting thorough searches to avoid trademark infringement and potential legal issues.

C. Legal Protection for Filmmakers

Understanding legal protections available for filmmakers is essential for navigating the industry confidently.

Legal Consultation and Representation

- **Early Legal Advice:** Seeking legal counsel at the early stages of the project to address potential legal challenges and mitigate risks.
- **Experienced Entertainment Attorneys:** Collaborating with legal professionals well-versed in entertainment law and film industry dynamics.

Insurance and Liability Coverage

- **Production Insurance:** Acquiring appropriate insurance to cover potential liabilities during production, including accidents, equipment damage, or other unforeseen events.
- **Error and Omission Insurance:** Obtaining E&O insurance to protect against legal claims related to copyright infringement, defamation, and other issues.

Contracts with Cast and Crew

- **Clear Employment Contracts:** Drafting contracts for cast and crew, specifying roles, responsibilities, compensation, and any clauses related to termination or non-disclosure.

- Protecting Creative Contributions: Ensuring contracts outline intellectual property ownership for work created during the project.

By understanding and addressing legal and contractual considerations, filmmakers can protect their rights, mitigate risks, and create a solid foundation for their film projects. From investor contracts to intellectual property protection and legal consultation, each aspect plays a crucial role in ensuring a smooth and legally sound journey through the film financing process.

Chapter X: Monetization Strategies Beyond Box Office

In this chapter, we will explore diverse revenue streams beyond traditional box office earnings that filmmakers can tap into to generate income and sustain their projects.

A. Exploring Various Revenue Streams

In the evolving landscape of the film industry, filmmakers have the opportunity to monetize their creations through a multitude of revenue streams. Understanding and strategically utilizing these streams is essential for long-term financial sustainability.

Streaming Platforms

- **Subscription Models:** Leveraging subscription-based platforms like Netflix, Hulu, or Amazon Prime, where viewers pay a recurring fee to access a library of films, providing a steady stream of revenue for filmmakers.
- **Pay-Per-View (PPV):** Partnering with streaming services for PPV releases, enabling audiences to pay to view the film for a limited time, often after its initial release.

DVD Sales and Rentals

- **Physical Sales:** Distributing DVDs of the film to retail outlets or selling directly to consumers online, particularly appealing to collectors or fans of physical media.

- Rental Platforms: Collaborating with online rental platforms like Redbox, allowing viewers to rent the film for a specified period, generating revenue through rentals.

Licensing

- Broadcast and Cable Licensing: Licensing the film to television networks or cable channels, generating revenue through broadcasting rights. This can involve licensing for a specific number of broadcasts or for a particular period.

- Educational Licensing: Licensing the film to educational institutions such as schools or universities, providing a valuable resource for classrooms and educational purposes, often through specialized educational distributors.

Merchandising and Branding

- Branded Merchandise: Creating and selling merchandise inspired by the film, such as apparel, accessories, or collectibles, extending the film's brand and generating additional income. This could be sold through various channels, including e-commerce websites, at screenings, or at events.

- Collaborations and Partnerships: Partnering with brands for co-branded merchandise, broadening the film's reach and diversifying revenue streams. This could include limited-edition merchandise featuring both the film and the brand.

International Sales

- International Distribution: Licensing the film to distributors in different countries, capitalizing on global markets and cultural diversity. Negotiating international distribution rights can lead to revenue from various territories around the world.

- Film Markets and Festivals: Showcasing the film at international film markets and festivals to attract international buyers and secure distribution deals. This exposure can lead to international sales and additional revenue streams.

Digital Downloads and VOD (Video on Demand)

- **Direct Sales:** Offering digital downloads through your website or online platforms, allowing viewers to purchase and own a digital copy of the film. This provides a convenient way for viewers to access the film and generates revenue through direct sales.
- **VOD Platforms:** Partnering with various VOD platforms to make the film available for online rental or purchase. These platforms often have a wide reach and can attract a broad audience.

B. Maximizing Revenue Potential

Strategic Release Planning

- **Optimal Release Timing:** Strategically planning release dates to align with market demand, festivals, or events, optimizing revenue potential. For example, releasing a horror film around Halloween or a family film during school holidays.
- **Cross-Platform Releases:** Coordinating releases across multiple revenue streams, ensuring a wider reach and maximizing earnings. This could involve releasing the film in theaters, on digital platforms, and on DVD simultaneously.

Marketing and Promotion

- **Targeted Marketing Campaigns:** Tailoring marketing efforts to specific revenue streams, effectively reaching the target audience for each stream. For example, focusing social media marketing on promoting merchandise to fans of the film.
- **Leveraging Social Media and Influencers:** Utilizing social media and influencers to promote the film and associated merchandise, driving sales and visibility. Collaborations with influencers who

align with the film's genre or target audience can be particularly effective.

Audience Engagement and Community Building

- **Building a Loyal Fanbase:** Engaging with the audience, cultivating a community of fans, and leveraging their support for ongoing projects and revenue generation. Engaged fans are more likely to support merchandise sales and future projects through crowdfunding or other funding models.
- **Crowdsourced Funding for Future Projects:** Utilizing the established fanbase to fund future projects through crowdfunding or pre-sales. Engaging with the audience and involving them in the filmmaking process can create a sense of ownership and encourage financial support for future endeavors.

Understanding and capitalizing on a diverse range of revenue streams is crucial for filmmakers seeking financial success beyond traditional box office earnings. By strategically exploring and maximizing these avenues, filmmakers can secure sustainable income to support their projects and fuel their creative endeavors.

Chapter XI: Insurance and Risk Management

In this chapter, we will delve into the crucial aspects of insurance and risk management for filmmakers, providing insights into various types of insurance to mitigate risks during film production.

A. Understanding Types of Insurance for Risk Mitigation during Production

Film production involves inherent risks, making insurance a critical tool for protecting investments, crew, equipment, and the overall project.

Production Insurance

- **Cast Insurance:** Protects against financial losses caused by delays or interruptions due to the incapacity, death, or other unforeseen circumstances involving key cast members. This coverage ensures the production can recover financially and continue in the event of unexpected circumstances affecting cast availability.
- **Production Package Insurance:** Offers comprehensive coverage for various risks during production, including property damage, equipment loss, and liability. It provides a broad safety net, covering a range of potential risks associated with filmmaking, thus ensuring financial security throughout the production process.

- **Weather Insurance:** Protects against financial losses incurred due to adverse weather conditions that impact the production schedule. This is particularly crucial for outdoor shoots and productions in regions with unpredictable weather patterns.

Liability Insurance

- **General Liability:** Covers third-party bodily injury or property damage claims that may arise during filming, such as accidents on set or damage to filming locations. This coverage is essential for protecting the production from legal claims that may occur during the filming process, offering financial support for potential legal costs and settlements.
- **Errors and Omissions (E&O) Insurance:** Protects against legal claims related to defamation, copyright infringement, or other intellectual property issues arising from the film's content. It safeguards the project against litigation that could arise from the content of the film, ensuring legal protection and financial support for potential legal challenges.

Equipment Insurance

- **Rented Equipment Insurance:** Provides coverage for equipment rented for the production, protecting against damage, loss, or theft. This coverage is crucial as it protects the production from financial losses associated with rented equipment, allowing the production to replace or repair vital equipment in case of damage or loss.
- **Owned Equipment Insurance**: Covers owned filming equipment, including cameras, lighting, and sound equipment, against various risks. This ensures that the production's investment in its equipment is protected, reducing financial risks associated with equipment damage, theft, or loss.

Post-Production Insurance

- Completion Bond: Guarantees the completion of the film according to the agreed-upon terms, offering protection to investors and financiers. A completion bond is a financial guarantee that provides assurance to investors that the film will be completed, reducing the risk associated with film production investments.

- Negative Film and Video Tape Insurance: Covers the loss or damage of original film negatives or digital footage during post-production. This insurance is critical in safeguarding the valuable footage and content that is essential for the completion of the film.

Travel and Health Insurance

- Travel Insurance: Provides coverage for crew and cast traveling for shoots, protecting against trip cancellations, delays, or medical emergencies. Travel insurance mitigates the financial risks associated with travel, ensuring that unexpected events do not disrupt the production schedule.

- Accident and Health Insurance: Offers coverage for medical expenses and accidents involving crew and cast during production. Health insurance protects the health and well-being of the team, providing financial support for medical care and related costs in case of accidents or health issues.

Cyber Insurance

- Cyber Liability Insurance: Protects against cyber threats and data breaches, which can be significant risks given the digital nature of modern film production and distribution. This insurance safeguards the production against potential cyber-attacks and data breaches, providing financial assistance for recovery and mitigating reputational risks.

Understanding the nuances of these insurance types and tailoring coverage based on the production's specific needs and risks is crucial for effective risk management and financial protection throughout the filmmaking process. Filmmakers should work closely with insurance professionals to design a comprehensive insurance strategy that aligns with the unique requirements of their production.

Chapter XII: Pre-visualization and Storyboarding

In this chapter, we will explore the significance of pre-visualization and storyboarding in the filmmaking process, illustrating their role in visualization, planning, and effective presentation of a film.

A. Utilizing Pre-visualization and Storyboarding for Visualization and Presentation

Pre-visualization (previs) and storyboarding are essential tools that provide filmmakers with a visual blueprint for their film, enabling effective planning, communication, and visualization of their creative vision.

Pre-visualization (Previs)

- **Digital Visualization:** Using computer-generated imagery (CGI) and specialized software to create a digital representation of the film, aiding in the planning of shots, sequences, and overall visual style. It helps in creating a rough, but accurate, representation of how the scenes will play out in the final film.
- **Benefit:**
    - **Enhanced Planning:** Allows filmmakers to plan camera movements, shot angles, and overall composition before actual production, optimizing efficiency and resources. Filmmakers can experiment with various creative ideas to find the most effective and compelling visual approach.

- **Communication Aid:** Helps in effectively communicating the director's vision to the entire production team, aligning everyone on the intended aesthetic and visual direction. This is especially crucial for complex scenes and sequences, ensuring a unified vision across the crew.
- **Budget Optimization:** Facilitates identifying and refining sequences to optimize the budget and resources required for complex scenes. By visualizing the scenes in advance, adjustments can be made to align with budget constraints without compromising the creative vision.

Storyboarding

- **Visualizing the Narrative:** Creating a sequence of hand-drawn or digitally generated illustrations that depict the shots and sequence of the film, offering a visual representation of the screenplay. It essentially tells the story visually, shot by shot.
- **Benefits:**
    - **Narrative Clarity:** Helps in organizing the narrative visually, ensuring coherence and flow in the storytelling. Filmmakers can identify pacing issues, gaps, or redundancies in the narrative through storyboarding.
    - **Visual Reference:** Provides a tangible visual reference for directors, cinematographers, and production teams to understand shot composition and progression. It allows for a clear visualization of how each shot contributes to the overall storytelling.
    - **Efficient Resource Allocation:** Facilitates resource allocation by providing insights into the number and types of shots needed for each scene. This information is critical for planning production schedules, set designs, and equipment requirements.

Integration and Collaboration

- Coordinating with Departments: Pre-visualization and storyboarding involve collaboration with various departments such as cinematography, production design, and visual effects to ensure alignment with the creative vision. It's a collaborative effort to ensure that the film's visual elements are cohesive and in line with the director's vision.

- Interactive Process: Encourages an iterative and collaborative process, allowing for feedback and adjustments to enhance the overall visual narrative. The iterative nature of pre-visualization and storyboarding allows for continuous improvement and refinement of the film's visual aspects.

Technological Advances

- Virtual Reality (VR) and Augmented Reality (AR): Utilizing VR and AR technologies to create immersive pre-visualization experiences, offering a more lifelike representation of scenes and sequences. VR and AR provide an immersive experience that can closely mimic how the final film will look and feel, aiding in better decision-making during pre-production.

- Real-Time Rendering: Leveraging real-time rendering engines to create interactive and dynamic previs, enabling instant adjustments and experimentation with different visual elements. Real-time rendering allows filmmakers to make quick decisions on lighting, camera angles, and more, improving the efficiency of the pre-visualization process.

Utilizing pre-visualization and storyboarding effectively empowers filmmakers to visualize their film in advance, plan shots and sequences strategically, enhance communication and collaboration within the production team, and optimize the efficient use of resources and budget.

Chapter XIII: Market Research and Audience Analysis

In this chapter, we will delve into the critical aspects of market research and audience analysis in the context of filmmaking, emphasizing the importance of understanding the target audience for a successful film production.

A. Conducting Market Research and Understanding the Target Audience

Market research and audience analysis are foundational steps in the filmmaking process, providing valuable insights that shape various aspects of the film, from its content to its marketing strategy.

Market Research

- **Defining the Market:** Identifying the target market for the film, considering demographics, geographic locations, and cultural preferences. Understanding the market landscape helps in tailoring the film to meet specific audience demands. For example, a film aimed at a younger, tech-savvy audience might incorporate digital marketing strategies and themes that resonate with this demographic.

- **Analyzing Trends and Competitors:** Studying trends in the film industry and analyzing competitors' successes and failures, extracting lessons and best practices to inform decision-making. Trends could indicate emerging genres or themes that are gaining popularity, enabling filmmakers to align their projects accordingly.
- **Budget Allocation and ROI Analysis:** Utilizing market research to allocate the budget effectively, focusing resources on aspects that resonate with the target market, thus optimizing return on investment (ROI). For instance, if the research shows a strong interest in visual effects, allocating a portion of the budget towards high-quality visuals may yield a higher ROI.

Understanding the Target Audience

- **Demographic Analysis:** Categorizing the potential audience based on age, gender, income levels, education, and other demographic factors to customize the film's content and promotional strategies accordingly. For example, a family-oriented film would be tailored to appeal to parents and children, considering appropriate themes and suitable viewing times.
- **Psychographic Profiling:** Delving into the psychographics of the audience, understanding their attitudes, values, lifestyles, and behaviors, allowing for a deeper understanding of their preferences and motivations. If the target audience values sustainability and eco-friendliness, incorporating these values into the film's message and marketing efforts can resonate effectively.
- **Consumer Behavior Insights:** Investigating how the target audience consumes media, their preferred platforms, and viewing habits to align the film's distribution and marketing strategies with their behavior. If the audience primarily consumes content via streaming platforms, prioritizing partnerships with these platforms for distribution would be strategic.

Feedback and Testing

- **Focus Groups and Surveys:** Conducting focus groups and surveys to gather direct feedback from potential viewers, providing valuable insights into their expectations and preferences. Feedback regarding plot elements, character development, or visual effects can guide necessary adjustments.
- **Test Screenings:** Organizing test screenings to gauge audience reactions, identify areas for improvement, and validate the film's appeal before its official release. Test screenings can provide critical insights into the audience's emotional responses, helping refine the final edit for maximum impact.

Tailoring the Film and Marketing Strategy

- **Content Customization:** Adapting the film's content, themes, characters, and storytelling to resonate with the identified target audience, ensuring a more engaging and relatable viewing experience. Customizing the narrative to address specific cultural nuances or societal concerns relevant to the audience can enhance engagement and connection.
- **Strategic Marketing and Promotion:** Tailoring marketing campaigns to reach the target audience effectively, selecting appropriate channels, messaging, and promotional tactics that align with their preferences and behavior. Utilizing influencers, targeting specific online platforms, or creating interactive marketing campaigns can be more effective when aligned with audience preferences.

Understanding the target audience through thorough market research enables filmmakers to make informed decisions about their film's content, marketing strategy, and distribution plan. By aligning the film with the audience's preferences and expectations, filmmakers increase the likelihood of success in the highly competitive film industry.

Chapter XIV: Film Festivals and Networking

In this chapter, we will delve into the importance of film festivals and networking events in the filmmaking industry, emphasizing their role in presenting opportunities for funding and growth.

A. Utilizing Film Festivals and Networking Events for Opportunities and Funding

Film festivals and networking events are crucial platforms for filmmakers to showcase their work, build valuable connections, and access funding opportunities.

Film Festivals

- **Showcasing Talent and Work**: Film festivals provide a platform to showcase films, attracting industry professionals, potential investors, and fellow filmmakers. This exposure can lead to recognition, distribution deals, or collaboration opportunities. Additionally, festivals often categorize films, making it easier for filmmakers to target festivals that align with their film's genre or theme, maximizing visibility.
- **Networking and Collaboration**: Filmmakers can connect with like-minded professionals, potential investors, and industry experts, fostering collaboration and partnerships for future projects. Collaborative efforts can lead to co-productions or

shared resources, reducing the financial burden on individual filmmakers.
- **Awards and Recognition:** Winning awards at film festivals can significantly boost a film's visibility and credibility, attracting further attention and potential financial support. Awards serve as a testament to the quality and creativity of the film, capturing the interest of investors and distributors.

Networking Events

- **Industry Connections:** Networking events offer a space to establish connections with producers, investors, distributors, and other professionals crucial for a film's success. Building a strong network opens doors to potential funding, co-production opportunities, and collaborations. Effective networking involves not only meeting industry professionals but also maintaining relationships through follow-ups and continued engagement.
- **Knowledge Sharing and Learning:** Attending panels, workshops, and discussions during networking events allows filmmakers to gain insights into industry trends, financing options, and successful strategies from seasoned professionals. This knowledge equips filmmakers with the information needed to navigate the complex world of film financing and production effectively.
- **Pitching and Presenting Projects:** Networking events often provide platforms to pitch film projects to potential investors and production companies. Filmmakers can seize these opportunities to secure funding and support for their films. Mastering the art of a compelling pitch is crucial in capturing the attention and interest of potential backers.

Crowdfunding and Fundraising Opportunities

- **Showcasing Projects to the Public:** Utilizing crowdfunding platforms at or around film festivals allows filmmakers to present their projects to a broad audience, attracting individual investors who are passionate about supporting independent cinema. Timing campaigns to coincide with a festival can generate excitement and enthusiasm among festival attendees.

- **Connecting with Supporters:** Engaging with potential backers during festivals and events can lead to increased visibility for crowdfunding campaigns, encouraging more supporters to contribute to the film. Interacting with the audience and sharing the film's vision can generate a sense of community support, driving crowdfunding success.

Film Marketplaces and Forums

- **Exploring Distribution and Sales:** Film markets within festivals provide opportunities for filmmakers to explore distribution and sales deals for their films. Connecting with distributors and sales agents can lead to successful commercial distribution, ensuring the film reaches a broader audience and generates revenue.
- **Seeking Co-Production and Financing Deals:** Forums often facilitate meetings and discussions for co-production and financing opportunities, connecting filmmakers with potential co-producers, financiers, and collaborators for their projects. These interactions can lead to partnerships that alleviate financial burdens and facilitate the production process.

Film festivals and networking events are essential components of the filmmaking journey, offering a myriad of opportunities to showcase talent, connect with industry professionals, and access funding for film projects. Harnessing the potential of these platforms requires strategic planning, effective networking skills, and a deep understanding of how to leverage each opportunity for the film's benefit.

Chapter XV: Digital Distribution and Online Platforms

In this chapter, we will explore the significance of digital distribution and online platforms in modern filmmaking, focusing on how filmmakers can leverage these avenues for audience engagement and revenue generation.

A. Leveraging Digital Distribution and Online Platforms for Audience Engagement and Revenue Generation

Digital distribution and online platforms have revolutionized the way films are shared with audiences and monetized. Understanding the dynamics of this landscape is crucial for filmmakers seeking to effectively reach their target audience and generate revenue.

Digital Distribution

- **Wide Reach and Accessibility:** Utilizing digital distribution allows filmmakers to reach a global audience, transcending geographical boundaries. Online platforms provide accessibility to a vast number of viewers, increasing the film's exposure and potential reach. From established platforms to independent websites, the internet offers numerous opportunities to showcase work to a diverse audience.

- Cost-Effectiveness: Digital distribution often eliminates the need for physical copies, reducing distribution costs significantly. This cost-effectiveness allows filmmakers to allocate resources to other essential aspects such as marketing and production quality.

Online Platforms

- Streaming Services: Leveraging established streaming platforms like Netflix, Amazon Prime Video, Hulu, and others can provide a massive audience base. Getting a film on one of these platforms can lead to substantial viewership and potential revenue through licensing deals or viewership-based payments. Understanding the submission and acquisition processes for these platforms is crucial for successful distribution.

- Video-on-Demand (VOD) Platforms: VOD platforms allow filmmakers to directly distribute and monetize their films. Platforms like Vimeo On Demand and YouTube Movies enable filmmakers to set pricing, reach a global audience, and retain a share of the revenue generated. Choosing the right platform and pricing strategy is essential for maximizing earnings and attracting viewers.

- Social Media and YouTube: Utilizing platforms like YouTube or social media channels allows for free or cost-effective distribution. Creating a channel for the film or promotional content can engage the audience and build anticipation for the release, leading to increased viewership. Utilizing effective SEO, engaging thumbnails, and consistent posting can boost visibility and subscriber growth.

Direct-to-Consumer (DTC) Models

- Building a Fanbase: Engaging with the audience directly through a dedicated website or online community can create a loyal fanbase. Offering exclusive content, merchandise, or early access to films can incentivize fans to support the filmmaker financially. Building a strong online presence through newsletters, blogs, or interactive live sessions can foster a community of engaged fans.

- Subscription Models: Implementing subscription-based models where viewers pay a regular fee for access to a filmmaker's content can provide a steady source of income. This model encourages consistent engagement and financial support from the audience. Balancing subscription costs with the perceived value of the content is crucial for maintaining a healthy subscriber base.

Monetization Strategies

- Pay-Per-View (PPV): Implementing a PPV model for online screenings or premieres allows filmmakers to monetize specific events. Fans can purchase a virtual ticket to watch the film during a limited screening period. Effective marketing and creating a sense of exclusivity can drive PPV sales.
- Ad Revenue and Sponsorships: Monetizing through ads on platforms like YouTube or sponsored content can generate revenue based on the number of views and engagement. Collaborating with brands or sponsors can also provide funding for the film or related content. Identifying appropriate sponsors aligned with the film's genre or message is essential for successful partnerships.
- Merchandise Sales: Offering branded merchandise related to the film, such as clothing, posters, or collectibles, can be a lucrative revenue stream. Fans often enjoy owning tangible items related to their favorite films. Designing appealing and unique merchandise and integrating it effectively into marketing strategies can drive sales.

Understanding how to effectively utilize digital distribution and online platforms empowers filmmakers to engage their audience, monetize their work, and establish a sustainable model for future projects. Utilizing a combination of these strategies, tailored to the film's genre, target audience, and unique value proposition, can maximize the film's visibility and revenue potential.

Chapter XVI: Ethical and Sustainable Financing Practices

In this chapter, we will explore the importance of ethical and sustainable financing practices within the film industry. We'll emphasize how filmmakers can promote responsible financial decisions that contribute to a more sustainable and equitable film landscape.

A. Promoting Ethical and Sustainable Financing Practices in the Film Industry

Ethical and sustainable financing practices in filmmaking involve making conscious financial decisions that prioritize not only the success of a film but also the well-being of stakeholders, the environment, and society at large.

Responsible Funding Sources

- Avoiding Exploitative Funding: Filmmakers should be cautious of funding sources that exploit artists or lead to unfair working conditions. This includes being aware of predatory lending practices, excessively high interest rates, or contracts that burden the filmmakers with unjust financial obligations. Ensuring funding sources align with ethical principles and do not compromise the welfare of those involved in the project is fundamental.

Fair Compensation and Rights

- Fair Pay and Treatment: Filmmakers should strive for fair compensation for all individuals involved in the production, including actors, crew members, and other contributors. Ensuring fair wages and working conditions contributes to a more ethical and sustainable film industry. Fair treatment fosters a positive work environment, enhancing creativity and productivity.

- Intellectual Property Rights: Filmmakers should understand and protect their intellectual property rights, ensuring that their creative work is valued and that they receive appropriate compensation for its use and distribution. Respecting intellectual property rights is essential for fostering a culture that values originality and creativity, ultimately benefiting the industry as a whole.

Transparent Financial Practices

- Financial Transparency: Filmmakers should maintain transparency in financial transactions and distribution of funds. Clear accounting and disclosure of how funds are allocated and spent within a film project foster trust and accountability among stakeholders. Transparency also builds credibility, attracting potential investors and collaborators who value honesty and openness.

Sustainable Production Practices

- Environmental Considerations: Filmmakers should strive for sustainable production practices that minimize the environmental impact of their projects. This can include reducing waste, minimizing carbon emissions, and adopting eco-friendly alternatives in production processes. Implementing sustainable practices not only aligns with global environmental goals but also sets a positive example for other industries.

- Supporting Sustainable Businesses: Filmmakers can prioritize working with vendors and suppliers who follow sustainable practices, thus promoting a more environmentally conscious supply chain within the industry. By supporting sustainable businesses, filmmakers contribute to a circular economy and encourage the adoption of responsible practices throughout the production process.

Social Responsibility

- Diversity and Inclusion: Filmmakers should advocate for diversity and inclusion in all aspects of filmmaking, including casting, crew selection, and storytelling. Embracing diverse perspectives not only enriches the film industry but also supports social equity and inclusivity. Inclusive storytelling reflects the richness of human experiences and fosters empathy and understanding.
- Community Engagement: Filmmakers can engage with local communities during production, respecting their cultural sensitivities and involving them in the filmmaking process when appropriate. This collaboration fosters positive relationships and community support for the industry. Engaging with communities ensures that filmmaking activities contribute positively to the social fabric of the regions involved.

Education and Awareness

- Promoting Financial Literacy: Filmmakers should advocate for and participate in initiatives that enhance financial literacy within the industry. Educating filmmakers about sound financial practices empowers them to make informed and ethical financial decisions throughout their careers. Financial literacy equips filmmakers with the tools to manage finances responsibly and navigate the complexities of funding and budgeting effectively.

Promoting ethical and sustainable financing practices in the film industry contributes to a more responsible and equitable ecosystem. Filmmakers have the power to influence positive change through their financial decisions, promoting a culture of fairness, transparency, and responsibility within the film community. By embracing ethical financing practices, filmmakers can create a more sustainable and inclusive film industry that benefits everyone involved.

Chapter XVII: Conclusion

In this concluding chapter, we revisit the essential aspects of financing and budgeting within the film industry. We emphasize the significance of making informed financial decisions, encouraging creativity in funding approaches, and fostering continuous learning and networking within the filmmaking community.

A. Reiterating the Importance of Proper Financing and Budgeting for Successful Film Projects

Financing and budgeting are the lifeblood of any film project. Without adequate and well-planned financing, a project may struggle to come to fruition or may face challenges during production, affecting the overall quality and success of the film. Proper budgeting ensures that resources are allocated judiciously, allowing for a smooth production process and a polished final product.

Understanding the financial landscape of the film industry, exploring various funding avenues, and developing a comprehensive budget are foundational steps for filmmakers. It is crucial to assess the financial needs of a project accurately and plan accordingly to secure the necessary funding to bring the creative vision to life.

B. Encouragement for Filmmakers to Explore Various Financing Options and Embrace Creativity in Funding Their Projects

The filmmaking landscape offers a plethora of financing options, ranging from traditional methods like grants, loans, and investors to modern approaches like crowdfunding, digital distribution, and online platforms. Filmmakers are encouraged to explore and leverage these diverse financing avenues.

Creativity in funding is as essential as creativity in storytelling. Thinking outside the box and devising innovative strategies to fund a film can lead to exciting opportunities and unique projects. Embrace creativity not only in your filmmaking but also in how you finance and market your work. Engage with your audience, tell your story compellingly, and consider novel ways to involve them in your journey.

C. Encouraging Continuous Learning and Networking within the Film Industry

In the ever-evolving film industry, continuous learning is paramount. Stay updated with the latest trends, technologies, and financing models by participating in workshops, seminars, and online courses. Networking with fellow filmmakers, industry professionals, and potential investors can provide invaluable insights and opportunities for collaboration and growth.

Filmmaking is a collaborative art form, and building a network of connections within the industry can open doors to financing, partnerships, and mentorship. Engage in meaningful conversations, seek guidance, and share your experiences. A supportive community can be instrumental in navigating the challenges and complexities of the film industry.

D. Celebrating the Filmmaking Journey

Each film is a testament to the dedication, passion, and creativity of its creators. As you embark on your filmmaking journey, embrace the process, learn from each experience, and celebrate the milestones along the way. Every project, whether big or small, contributes to your growth as a filmmaker and enriches the tapestry of cinema.

E. Final Thoughts

Mastering the art of film financing and budgeting is a journey that requires dedication, creativity, and a keen business sense. As a filmmaker, you possess the power to turn your visions into reality, and financial acumen is a crucial tool on this path. Remember, every film project is a story in itself—a story of perseverance, creativity, and the collaborative spirit of the filmmaking community.

By delving into the intricacies of financing, embracing creativity in funding approaches, and building a strong network of collaborators and supporters, you set the stage for a success.

In the world of filmmaking, where dreams become images, creativity knows no bounds, and every frame is a canvas of infinite possibilities, remember that your journey has only just begun.

The world eagerly awaits your stories, so may your passion continue to fuel your cinematic odyssey, and may your films forever illuminate the screen and touch the hearts of countless souls.

Stay inspired. Stay creative. Happy filmmaking!

About The Author

Chris Grant Wenchell is an American film and TV actor with a passion for storytelling and performance. He has made a significant impact on the world of entertainment, particularly in the vibrant landscape of indie films and television.

Notable roles include his portrayal of a sinister college student with unique powers in the TV series "Olympia." He has also taken on challenging characters in projects like "Charlie and Jimmy," "Writers Block Painting with the Devil," and "The Son Rises." Chris's latest achievement was starring in the thrilling sci-fi feature "Megalodon Rising," where he played a Tactical Action Officer on a Navy ship battling Megalodon sharks under the direction of Brian Nowak and the production of The Asylum.

In his recent television endeavors, Chris guest starred as Arson Gallegos, an ex-con running a chop shop, in "FBI: Most Wanted." He also co-starred in "The Rookie" as the crooked cop Rick Croyer.

In addition to his acting work, Chris has made his mark as a producer, overseeing various projects under his production company, XXII Pictures, including "Five Card Draw," "The Ordeal," "Dirt," and "Kingfish."

Chris Grant Wenchell's captivating presence and dedication to the world of film and television continue to shine in his artistic journey.

NOTES

NOTES

NOTES

NOTES

NOTES

NOTES